The
Advent
Remedy

Peter Traben Haas

CONTEMPLATIVE
CHRISTIANS.COM

Published by //
ContemplativeChristians.com

First Printing: November 2019

P.O. Box 164202
Austin, TX 78716

*The Advent Remedy: A Contemplative Daily
Reader for Advent and Christmas*

Library of Congress Cataloging-in-publication
Data

Haas, Peter Traben (1972 –   )

ISBN: 978-0-578-61170-9

Spirituality – Christianity. 2. Contemplative. 3.
Advent. I. Title.

The
Advent
Remedy

"We must close our eyes and invoke a new manner of seeing...A wakefulness that is the birthright of us all, though few put it to use."

- Plotinus

Welcome to the Advent Remedy

During this season, I invite you to keep a kind of *visual divina* Vigil during the evenings of Advent. The invitation is to, as you are able, watch the Light and let the Light watch you from sunset through dusk to dark. Be still. Listen. Watch. Wait.

Such a practice can supplement, and even infuse one's Centering Prayer practice with a deepened consent. To be still and simply watch the Light with "soft eyes" - seeking nothing other than simply being present to the movement of the Light's fading grace, night by night, as we move toward Winter Solstice, and of course the celebration Christmas, and shortly thereafter, Epiphany.

As we watch the fading Light together, it is possible we create a "field of Vigil devotion". In this field of devotion, we can feel and become more aware of the wholeness of our connected community of God-lovers in the Advent stillness and silence.

Perhaps one contemplative approach to the invitation to "prepare for the Light" is to acknowledge the reality of the shadows and darkness in our world and in our life and body-mind, and especially in each of our consciousness and unconsciousness. So, to prepare for the Light is to ask of ourselves "What in us is in need of being met, embraced, integrated and healed by the Light?" Sometimes the first step in preparing for the Light is to see the need for the Light's healing and guidance, at deeper and deeper and subtler places within us.

We also prepare for the Light in solidarity with our Jewish brothers and sisters, who celebrate Hanukkah in this season, a festival of Lights, observed by lighting the Nine candles of the Menorah.

In ancient Christianity a hymn was sung to help prepare for the Light, especially during the evening Vespers service. In Greek, it is called the *Phos Hilaron* and in Latin, *Lumen Hilare*, both meaning something like "O Gentle Light", or "O Gladsome Light". Here is one translation by William Storey:

O radiant light, O sun divine
Of God the Father's deathless face,
O image of the light sublime
That fills the heav'nly dwelling place.

O Son of God, the source of life,
Praise is your due by night and day;
Our happy lips must raise the strain
Of your esteemed and splendid name.

Lord Jesus Christ, as daylight fades,
As shine the lights of eventide,
We praise the Father with the Son,
The Spirit blest and with them one.

I wish you and your beloveds a most
Blessed Advent Vigil preparing and watching and even listening for the Light in the
silence. May the Adevent remedy bring you
deep peace, joy and love.

Monday of the First Week of Advent

I grew up mostly in Wisconsin, so I am used to Advent being cold, grey and snowy. Now, living in central Texas, we do sometimes get chilly days in Advent. Mostly, though, we just get big, cloudy days — that look cold — but actually are fairly mild, even warm. The big clouds rise up from the Gulf, just a two-hour drive to the south.

So, I often pretend it's cold. Yesterday was one of those days — the clouds looked like northern clouds, even though it was seventy-eight degrees by three in the afternoon. Another difference about a southern Advent is that the leaves on most of the trees are still green at Thanksgiving.

But, soon after, in these parts, we too can expect some autumnal color and change. And by Christmas week, we usually get a strong cold front coming down from Canada, unhindered by the flat plain states to the north of Texas; that end of year wind typically dismounts all remaining leaves, except, of course, the live oaks and the junipers.

Advent is a remedy. It's a four-fold count of grace, spinning us body and soul, deeper into the inner space of silence, where like a pool of stillness, the light of love touches our tongue with cleansing fire, so to speak and be spoken to with a goodness that heals.

A goodness that soaks into and releases even the earliest painful soul-stains. The stain isn't us. It just seems to mark us deeply, perhaps even never go away. What can remove this stain of pain? The remedy of Advent, which reveals and reminds us of our essential goodness.

That utmost inner gift of God to self. You are beautiful. You are good. You are loved. And that which in you is loved is goodness itself since nothing can separate it from the love of God in Christ.

The remedy of Advent heals even the deepest shadows of our being, where the pain still lingers, like a frozen bruise, blinding us to the deeper goodness hiding under the pain.

We tend to be strangers to such goodness, so it surprises us when we feel it up-surging through the cracks of beauty that Advent can awaken us to. We might even cry as the beauty and goodness come close, since our body and mental system don't know how to process it. Advent is so tactile. So embodied. Its beauty helps us feel. The songs. The lights.

The well-lighted wreath that leads us week by week down the hallway of an ancient time, keeping its appointment to each of us, so to heal us a little bit more. These are all helpers to our healing. A helpful easing of the cramp that comes with being so self-bound and wound. A healing that reveals the original goodness, hidden under the shadows of our shame and pain.

I'm writing in the darkness of an early morning. It's the very beginning of the Advent journey. I have no destination. All I know is that words somehow keep helping me light the way. A way imbued with the Word. I've spent a good portion of my lifetime chasing and being chased by this Word.

Only in the silence, jumping in bare to the soul, have I discovered that the Word is more than any book; more than any earth or universe; more than any light or darkness. It is the Word beyond all words – that only silence can unwrap with its wisdom.

I don't need to understand it. I welcome being understood by it, though. This is a contemplative speaking. And this shall be a contemplative Advent – perhaps an untired remedy for the severe swings drawing our attention between chaos and peace, heaven and earth, right and left, campaign and election, count and re-count, up and down, light and darkness…and everything in between.

Let's take the Advent remedy together.

Tuesday of the First Week of Advent

*"On that day, A shoot shall sprout from the stump
of Jesse, and from his roots a bud shall blossom.
The Spirit of the LORD shall rest upon him: a
Spirit of wisdom and of understanding, A Spirit of
counsel and of strength, a Spirit of knowledge and of
fear of the LORD..."*
– Isaiah 11. 1 – 2

In Peter Wohlleben's enchanting book, *The
Hidden Life of Trees*, he tells a story of walk-
ing through the forest he manages in Ger-
many and discovering what appeared to be
moss-covered rocks. Upon further explora-
tion, he realized that the "stones" were actually small living stumps, forming the pe-
riphery of a large rotted out tree stump,
felled over five hundred years ago.

Though the tree was long dead, with no living root system for nutrient delivery, or
leaves for photosynthesis, somehow the
small stump cluster was alive!

When Wohlleben cut into them, the wood
was green with chlorophyll.

This unexpected discovery helped him realize that somehow the root system of nearby beach trees were giving the old, felled tree some of their nutrients by way of their intertwined roots. Perhaps the beach trees actually loved the old majestic tree and missed it?

We are discovering that all of creation is relational – more like a social network than a cog in a machine. The whole is superabundant to the parts. And the parts are superabundant to the whole. Interrelated is the key word. Harmonious. Loving. Self-giving. Inter-being.

From nature and its living systems, we can gain insight as to what the sprout off the stump of Jesse might be. The sprout symbolizes the Presence of Life itself. The stump is the past – God's legacy with previous generations. The sprout is Life – and its unfolding will toward evolutionary love and human development into Christ. It is new Life that is emerging forth from the stump of God's prior work and activity among humankind.

We are participants in this process of unfolding Life. We are Spirit embodied beings unfolding, generation by generation, toward the fullness of Christ, which is, in a certain sense, the Tree of Life and the Tree of Knowledge. The contrast between the past and the future is that much development occurs in between.

Allegorically, the past and early levels of our human development are represented by the Garden, where the "trees" once flourished. They represent our innocence and more primitive behaviors such as shame, fear and violence; all behaviors which also still lurk in our present.

The future and our potential future human development is represented by the City of God, where the trees will flourish in the fullness of light, which represents wisdom – as well as Divine Presence – which includes us. Another way of saying that, is that we are becoming a universe of love, intertwined together by the force and motion of Life Itself – deeper forward toward the Body of Christ (1 Cor 15.28).

As for the practical, in our day to day life, notice where you feel dead inside and request help from Life and Love to nurture and support you, to come along side of you and intertwine Love's roots with your human root system – and be renewed by the Remedy of Advent Life.

This might require letting go of other roots that choke out life – the deadness of entertainment, gluttony, laziness, drunkenness and other such distractions that limit your flourishing. You know the difference.

You were not created to be a cut down stump. You are here to flourish- and the mystery is – in God's love-life-energy, we can and do flourish, even as we are dying. Remember, Advent always leads to Holy Week's paradoxical hosanna: "into thy hands I commit my spirit."

Wednesday of the First Week of Advent

"The law of the LORD is perfect, refreshing the soul..."
—Psalm 19.8

So begins a Psalm to remember, and often call to mind in the heart. It is a teaching-Psalm that indicates the remedies available to us as we ponder the written Word of God in Scripture.

Notice the remedies provided through this important influence of scripture:

Gives wisdom.

Brings joy to the emotional center (i.e., heart).

Brings enlightenment to one's perception or reality.

Brings the capacity to do (possessing wealth).

Brings deep satisfaction (sweeter than honey).

Rumi's poem, *The Waterwheel,* helps me remember how the written word of God flows and infuses a community to hear and share the Living Word of God together.

In this poem, I take the waterwheel to be the written "book", and the water to be the wisdom of Scripture flowing through the written words: Stay together, friends, Don't scatter and sleep. Our friendship is made of being awake. The waterwheel accepts water and turns and gives it away, weeping…Stay here, quivering with each moment like a drop of mercury.*

The remedy of Advent comes to us in many ways. Beauty. Lights. Carols. Family. And especially through the waterwheel of the scriptures flowing to us, weaving us day by day, Sunday by Sunday into a community of wisdom and love together.

*From The Essential Rumi Translated by Coleman Barks (New York: Harper Collins San Francisco, 1995) 247.

Thursday of the First Week of Advent

"The LORD is God, and he has given us light."
– Psalm 118.27a

The word "December" comes from the Latin *dece*, meaning ten. For generations prior to 700 CE, the Roman calendar only had ten months, culminating with December – the tenth month.

In both hemispheres of our planet, December is the month that marks the extent of light. In the Northern, the Winter Solstice on December 21st, marks the longest night of the year, and in the Southern, the opposite happens: it's the Summer Solstice on December 21st, marking the shortest night of the year.

Advent is a season of preparing for the coming of the Light. Not just the earthly experience of sunlight, marked by the calendar and the procession of the earth around the sun, but also the coming of the Light of the World – the presence of Christ: in history, in our present moment, in the future, and especially in the Eucharist.

I enjoy and perceive the fading light of
these December days. It helps me remember
the gift of life made possible by light,
and also to direct my attention inwardly to
wisdom, symbolized as light.

I find that the quality of December light —
its slanting rays more diffused lower on the
horizon and framed by bare trees — helps
me feel subtle impressions upon my emotional
center. The cold of December also
draws me inward, toward my heart — and all
of this combined, supports our communal
experience of waiting, watching and wondering
for the Light.

Friday of the First Week of Advent

"Thus says the Lord GOD: But a very little while, and Lebanon shall be changed into an orchard, and the orchard be regarded as a forest! On that day the deaf shall hear the words of a book; And out of gloom and darkness, the eyes of the blind shall see."
– Isaiah 29.17 – 18

The remedy of Advent is transformative. Life-contrasts and tensions resolve like a minor chord in the turning process of our attention, one week at a time – deeper toward the Christ mass – which is a density of grace and an intensity of love that can't be understood, but can be attended to, indeed, even nurtured.

The receptivity of the divine density and intensity is what prompts the transformation. And notice also that the transformation is developmental; that is to say, grace doesn't often happen all it once. It unfolds. Emerges. Evolves:

From a barren land, to an orchard, to a forest.

From unhearing, to hearing, to the book.

From gloom, to darkness, to seeing.

What are you giving your attention to? The barrenness? The unhearing ignorance and cacophony of cultural noise and conflict? The gloom and darkness of life on this planet under the influences of heavy unconscious forces? Or, perhaps to the forest? The book? The seeing process of contemplation?

Saturday and Sunday of the First Week of Advent

"The light of the moon will be like that of the sun and the light of the sun will be seven times greater like the light of seven days. On the day the LORD binds up the wounds of his people, he will heal the bruises left by his blows."
– Isaiah 30.26

When it comes to the biblical prophets, such as Isaiah, and when it comes to the prophetic genre overall, we often get glimpses of the significant role cosmology plays in spirituality. If you doubt this, just read the book of Revelation.

In this passage from the Prophet Isaiah above, we see a hint that the universe, and especially our line of planets stemming off our sun – is developmental. Thus, time is involved. As time seems to unfold, possible development might also occur.

But time and development are not guaranteed. Much time can pass with little development. Likewise, much development can occur in a short amount of time.

The image of the moon developing into a sun and the sun developing into a super-sun isn't that far-fetched. I have read elsewhere that some even think the earth will become a sun to the moon on the moon's developmental journey into becoming a living planet. No doubt there is much to ponder as we look up into the heavens.

The heavens are declaring and revealing much about our possibilities as a species on this planet. Perhaps it is wise just to say this: Christianity can't be unwoven from cosmology. They need to be paired, and any Christianity without a cosmology is incomplete.

On a more personal, practical and present level, the Advent Remedy can be seen here in the binding of the wounds. In the grace of an Advent journey, something can happen to us inwardly that helps us move into a deeper wholeness, healing our inner fragmentation and transforming us into a more complete, developed Being.

Suffering seems to be a part of this transformation process of development. In Christian terms, crucifixion leads to resurrection and resurrection leads to ascension – until we reach the full stature of Christ

Note also that the prophets of Israel spoke their wisdom and words in the midst of great national and personal suffering, loss and discontinuity. It's no wonder that wave after wave of these prophetic texts announces a future deliverance, healing and restoration – whether through the idealized office of a King in the of David, or through the direct intervention of Israel's God.

Nevertheless, Israel's hope (and now ours) was (and is) directed toward the unfolding future. This presents some challenges on the spiritual level if the hope gets uprooted from simply being present in the Presence.

On the other hand, without hope, and without the unfolding future emerging in cooperation with our participation, our spiritual life often coils and caves into a distorted narcissism of the moment – and flat-lines the dynamic movement of the Spirit that is Life itself birthing newness from a hidden love toward an unknown love that wishes to us as its partner, in this life and beyond.

I guess the best way to apply such mysteries, is this:

Don't give up.

Whatever is happening in and to your life, use it as fuel for transformation. Keep moving toward the emergent love of God coming toward you. Somewhere, somehow It meets us and heals us from one degree of glory to the next – until we are all "suns" of God in the Wholeness of the Resurrected Christ.

Monday of the Second Week of Advent

"One day as Jesus was teaching, Pharisees and teachers of the law, who had come from every village of Galilee and Judea and Jerusalem, were sitting there, and the power of the Lord was with him for healing. And some men brought on a stretcher a man who was paralyzed…"
– Luke 5.17 – 18

"He stood up immediately before them, picked up what he had been lying on, and went home, glorifying God."
– Luke 5.25

Two aspects of this famous passage arose to my attention today, in a way I had never before seen.

First, notice that the "power of the Lord" was with Jesus. And the healing is attributed in essence to this power working through Jesus. Such instances are indications of the anointedness of Jesus. In the Jewish context, the power of the Lord was conveyed by the anointing of oil upon the head of a prophet, priest or king – empowering them for a specific task or ministry.

In this case, we see that the anointing of Jesus went beyond oil – and was consummated by the anointing of Jesus by the power of the Holy Spirit symbolized by the dove at his baptism.

The anointing that brings the power of the Lord is spiritually important because it is the fact that Jesus is anointed that makes him the Christ. Keep in mind that the Greek word *christos* (Christ) was used to translate the Hebrew word מָשִׁיחַ (messiah), which literally means, "anointed one." Jesus was anointed with power to heal by the Spirit of God – a power that continues to be available for us.

Second, the paralyzed man not only stands up and is healed but picks up his past and goes home glorifying God. The "picking up what he had been lying on" is a small but significant detail of the story. Perhaps it shows that it takes time to release the past – as if he can't believe that he has been healed. Or, that perhaps he fears the paralysis will return and he will need the cot he was laying on again.

Or, even more striking, perhaps the cot represents that which he is most ashamed of. He takes it with him so that no one will see it and remember who he was. I can imagine him throwing the cot and linens away – even burning them. Releasing them when he finally realizes that he is no longer bound by his previous way of being that has so captivated him for so many years.

In this sense, I find deep resonance with our human patterns of behavior that do not serve our flourishing – that keep us paralyzed to further potential and possibility. Addictions. Patterns of reacting. Negative thoughts. Violence. Negative feelings, and so on.

Such are a few aspects of the Remedy of Advent: the healing power of the Spirit of God anointing not only Jesus, but Mary, the early church and continuing toward our lives today and beyond. And the invitation to receive the healing and be freed but also instructed by our past, especially the past we may be most ashamed of.

The power of our healing includes an integrating grace that brings a degree of peace and acceptance of who and what we have been. We take it with us not to hide it or deny it in shame, but to integrate it for our ongoing journey into wholeness and Realness. And as we do, it's amazing how our healing may help others heal.

Tuesday of the Second Week of Advent

"Comfort, give comfort to my people, says your God. Speak tenderly to Jerusalem…"
– Isaiah 40.1

These famous words of the prophet Isaiah resound in churches during Advent. Perhaps made more famous since they feature prominently in Handel's Messiah, a perennial favorite this time of year. Apart from their poetic power, the prophet's words speak to a deep need and wish, something I refer to as the Advent Remedy.

The Advent Remedy can heal the contrasts and eases the friction-points of our life. The Advent Remedy reverses wrongs and inaugurates rights. The Advent Remedy invites to mature beyond the misperceptions of duality toward the understanding of union.

The Advent Remedy is that revelation and application of the Christ-Union, wedding human and divine. This ongoing remedy — and our attention to it and participation in it — is what ultimately brings comfort to people: the easing of resentment; the release of guilt and shame; the reconciliation between our longings and reality; the awakening of wisdom. Such are a few of the gifts of the Advent Remedy.

The Advent Remedy isn't one and done. It's a lifetime journey. Year by year, we take the four-fold count of the Advent Sundays as a rhythm of grace to live by. Deeper than just remembering the birth of the "baby Jesus" the Advent Remedy reminds us that Jesus invites us to go where he went. Deeper into the Union.

And yet Union is just the start! No need to build a museum at Christmas and enshrine Jesus there forever. The remedy moves deeper.

Indeed, there are other remedies beyond Advent – such as Easter, Ascension and Pentecost, which reveal something beyond Union – perhaps something that is Pure Mystery: the realities of Christ. Trinity. Life in the Spirit. And Theosis – the ultimate remedy of all.

And last but not least. Probably, any comfort we receive in life will somewhere, somehow also involve a cross. It's quantum joy and suffering all the way. Or, in theological terms: cross and resurrection.

Wednesday of the Second Week of Advent

"Jesus said to the crowds: 'Come to me, all you who labor and are burdened, and I will give you rest. Take my yoke upon you and learn from me, for I am meek and humble of heart; and you will find rest for yourselves. For my yoke is easy, and my burden light.'"
– Matthew 11.28 – 30

Among the many beloved verses in the Gospels, this must be one of the most cherished. Its devotional quality is self-evident. I begin every funeral service with these words and have often repeated them to myself and others during highly stressful situations and seasons in life.

In this passage, the Advent Remedy is once again revealed. If we apply the invitation inwardly, the "crowd" is within. Our fragmentation. Our multiplicity. Our non-integrated ways of being. This is the crowd that needs to attend to the Center. And we can all use a break from that interior chaos, confusion and disorder. The question is how?

One answer is that first, the personal pronoun "me", needs to be interpreted. In the narrative context, obviously, this "me" is Jesus. He literally meant "come to me – right now. From where you are standing there, to here."

Such an invitation made sense with him standing right there, inviting the crowd to follow him, versus disperse and go their own ways.

Second, let's admit that in this moment, today, Jesus is not standing right here. The physical, historical Jesus, truthfully, is literally nowhere to be found. While it is a nice devotional sentiment that Jesus walks with me and he talks with me, I would invite us to be more truthful about our spiritual expressions and experiences.

The truth is that very, very, very few people can say that Jesus is right here with them as a historical person and physical presence – even as a resurrected body (yes, three very's!)

So, in Jesus' physical absence, how might this passage of scripture be applied more truthfully for each of us as a part of the Advent Remedy?

One suggestion is to replace the pronoun "me" with the word "center." Thus:

Come to the Center...and the Center will
give you rest.

Return to the Center...and learn...
for the Center is meek and humble of heart;

and you will find rest for yourselves.

For the Center is easy...light.

The Center is Christ. The circumference,
our life.

As Mr. Gurdjieff once said, for Christmas I give you Christ. Center comes to circumference.

Another idea is to replace the pronoun "me" with the word Eucharist. Thus:

Come to the Eucharist…

and the Presence will give you rest.

Return to the Eucharist…

and learn…

for the Eucharist is meek and humble of heart;

and you will find rest for yourselves.

For the Eucharist is easy…light.

And, there is more. Other ideas to replace the personal pronoun might be: Spirit. Silence. Or Stillness. All of them convey the Presence of Christ beyond the time-bound and ascended Jesus. And doing so helps us more realistically and truthfully experience the Advent Remedy.

Thursday of the Second Week of Advent

"...nothing will be impossible for God. Mary said, 'Behold, I am the handmaid of the Lord. May it be done in me by means of your word.'"
– Luke 1. 37-38

Mary features prominently in the Christmas story. Among other things, she is certainly the primary witness to the spiritual principle of receptivity to the new, not to be stopped evolution of God's love among us, indeed through us.

I translated the last verse a little differently to help bring out the nuance of her receptivity. I love Thomas Keating's word for this: Consent. Consenting is what we do beyond our receptivity.

I also have always appreciated Francis Schaeffer's insight on this passage as well, which can be found in his book True Spirituality. Schaeffer calls this principle of spiritual receptivity active-passivity. The pairing of both Mary's active Yes and Mary's passive consent to the Word.

May it be done in me by means of your word. I find this to be the essence of prayer, and an invitation to each of us on the spiritual journey to learn from Mary.

Friday of the Second Week of Advent

"Jesus said to the crowds: 'To what shall I compare this generation? It is like children who sit in marketplaces and call to one another, We played the flute for you, but you did not dance...'"
– Matthew 11. 16-17

The Advent Remedy helps us with our addiction to distraction. The human generations that come and go, decade by decade and century by century, have grown increasingly distracted. It is easy to spot this culturally. It may be more challenging to admit it personally.

The four-fold pattern of weeks between Thanksgiving and Christmas is the season of Advent. It is intended to be a remedy for our distraction, not a further contribution to it.

That is one reason why Advent is an ideal time to take a brief retreat away your daily routine.

Perhaps even a multi-day Centering Prayer retreat. Such retreats allow us to notice and correct how distracted we've become. The remedy is received simply by slowing down and settling into the winter stillness. It is good for the soul and the body.

When I can't take a retreat, I aim each day during Advent to take a break around the hour of sunset – to watch the fading light deepen into the violet darkness.

There is a special quality to the light of December as it nears the Winter solstice, and this light-quality helps me remember, helps me collect myself, helps me ease out of my often distracted, commuting state and consent to feeling the Loving Presence of Love in the silent stillness.

To my heart, Advent is simply another way of saying and being Contemplative.

Saturday and Sunday of the Second Week of Advent

"In those days, like a fire there appeared the prophet Elijah whose words were as a flaming furnace."
– Sirach 48.1

I'm writing beside our fireplace on this chilly central Texas morning. The fire is roaring – stoked with oak and pinion wood and lit by birch kindling and chunks of cardboard I re-purposed from old U-Haul moving boxes that hauled my books from Iowa to Texas two years ago. The fire has been a warm companion during the early, dark hours of this Second Saturday of Advent.

A cold front moved through the region Thursday bringing the coldest temperatures of the year – 31 degrees. I know that's not cold compared to other places, but for the Texas Hill country – it is. It's a shock to the system and reminds me just how important warmth is for our survival.

Sitting by my fire this morning, I read of the fire of Elijah. His story arises to our attention in the remembrance of the lectionary reading noted above, as a connecting witness to the presence and ministry of John the Baptist, who again features prominently in tomorrow's Gospel reading.

Whose words were a flaming furnace. What a statement. Fire represents not only the warmth of God's love but also the transforming power of God's Spirit of Wisdom. Fire and light are symbols of consciousness and wisdom.

Elijah clearly represents a deeper, higher level of wisdom and consciousness – a level that transcends our ordinary dimensions of existence, and that has something to do to with his own ascension.

Elijah, like John the Baptist, are types. They are Witness-bearers. They are tabernacles of the burning Light of Wisdom and Love, calling to the people, often made cold by their forgetfulness of the Light and Love of God, to be re-kindled. To Remember. To Be. And to Become.

If this dimension of Fire is missing from your Advent and Christmas. If this season has become depleting and feels like a soggy blanket of fog, dulling your senses and heart with busyness, travel, shopping and stress, perhaps today is the day to take a moment and light your own fire.

You can do that by listening to the Word of God in small chunks, reading it over multiple times. This is called the practice of *lectio divina*.

And, what is more miraculous than lighting your own fire, is the grace of being lit by the fire of divine love in the silence of meditative prayer. We are lit to burn. We burn to become fire. We burn to serve. We serve to die. We die to be born to deeper and deeper dimensions of the light, life and love of God that is Christ.

Thomas Merton ends his life journey, The Seven Story Mountain, with these lines, as if spoken by God, and I close our reflection today with them in the spirit of our forerunner prophets of the Light, our suffering brothers, our burning fathers, Elijah and John:

"That you may become the brother of God and learn to know the Christ of the burnt men."''

Monday of the Third Week of Advent

"Silence, all people, in the presence of the LORD, who stirs forth from his holy dwelling."
– Zechariah 2.17

The lectionary readings today again focus on Mary. It's not a coincidence. As we move through Advent, the daily scripture readings of the lectionary move deeper through the cast of characters, sometimes returning multiple times to the Christmas story's main actors, such as Mary.

Similarly, John the Baptist also features prominently in the build up to Christmas, as do the prophecies of Isaiah. In many ways, Advent belongs to Mary and John. Their roles are paired and parallel in purpose in witness to the birth of Christ.

On a practical level, Mary is a symbol for the interior life of each human that receives Spirit of God, combines with it, and speaks forth the birth of a new and unique word of life and wisdom to others.

Silence plays an important role in attending to the Presence and discovering more about our own inner holy dwelling. Silence is often the womb in which the word of wisdom is combined with, stirred up and emerges forth from interior contemplation to exterior expression(s).

As we enter into the third week of Advent, take time to simply be in stillness with the silence, and let the silence be with you. The silence is the environment in which you can feel the Presence and Action of the Spirit of God stirring within.

Perhaps you can find a place of solitude or beauty that helps you remember that you are the holy dwelling.

Tuesday of the Third Week of Advent

"Thus says the LORD: Woe to the city, rebellious and polluted, to the tyrannical city! She hears no voice, accepts no correction; In the LORD she has not trusted, to God, she has not drawn near."
– Zephaniah 3.1 – 2

Amid the pleasantries and pageantry of the Advent and Christmas season, it's good to hear the edge of wisdom slice into the heart of resistance and give us a shock.

Take the Advent Remedy gently but notice its severity.

We are the city. I am the city. The city is within. Teeming with my multiplicity of personality. The me-dynamics are often hidden but can be revealed suddenly by a new situation I did not expect: Someone angry. Someone yelling at me. Something breaks.

Something doesn't go as I expected – and then, suddenly, like clouds parting – a whole new situation is revealed within me. A situation of emotion. A situation of thoughts. An inner tumult. A city of dynamics within – rebellious, disordered, resistant. Me without grace. Me without remembering. Me without love. Me without presence. Me with reactivity. Me with negativity. Me with fear. Me with wanting. And so on.

Such moments of multiplicity occur not to accuse or bring shame or guilt, but to reveal that in me which still needs to be healed and incorporated into the city of God – which is wholeness birthed in loving wisdom. That in me, which is still lost and unguided, in need of a shepherd to bring me back to Center.

Thankfully the inner city isn't always tyrannical! It's often quite calm and peaceful. At ease. Open to God. Open to love. Listening. Remembering.

Notice the contrast. Use the contrast in how you feel to keep humble. To keep working on yourself in the shade of Grace, as Love keeps working on you in its light.

For far too long, religion has been an excuse to be tyrannical toward others in the name of some God. In some cases, even tyrannical toward the self – body, soul and spirit.

We are to evolve beyond such distortions and toward the power, joy and freedom of wholeness in love. A love that dissolves fear, and its insidious dynamics that lead to separation and splitting – one from another, and one from oneself.

In the stillness and silence of meditative prayer, we re-discover the Advent Remedy healing us from the fears that lead to our own, inner disorder. As we are healed, little by little, we help each other remedy and live in the light of love not the darkness of fear.

Wednesday of the Third Week of Advent

"I form the light, and create the darkness..."
– Isaiah 45.6

Light is life.

For example, on planet earth, light makes life as we know it possible. If the sun died and suddenly ceased blazing, about eight minutes later the earth and life as we know it here would also begin a rapid descent into a frozen death.

Thankfully, that is unlikely to happen – at least not for billions of years. And by then, perhaps another Sun would have emerged. But the point of the example is to develop by way of analogy the significance of light. Physical light. And by analogy, spiritual light.

In Christianity, light is a symbol for God, consciousness, Christ and wisdom, to name a few. The analogy is all the more profound given the central importance of light to life on planet earth.

Thus, it is no wonder that our ancestors in the Northern Hemisphere noticed the significance of light at this time of year. The Winter Solstice marks the sun's farthest descent southward, nearing the southern horizon; even disappearing altogether from sight in some northern latitudes.

Having noticed the importance of light – both literally and anagogical – now also notice that light does not create itself. Light has a Source. The light is the medium by which we know and feel the Source. Light points us back to the Source.

In a certain sense, our human journey and experience is primarily limited to the light and the darkness. Beyond both, is God. Hidden Source. Unknowable apart from the light and darkness – at least while we are here, alive on earth.

Even as we wander, suffer and die on our journeys here on earth, we also can remember and rejoice that we are also a people of the light, from the light, for the light. We awaken more to its Source as we receive the light.

The earth and its relationship to the Sun are here to reveal the unrepeatable. To point to the Source beyond the light and the darkness, which is constantly calling to us through the light and the darkness, to grope, to seek, to be quickened and warmed and take our journey beyond light and darkness with total faith.

Thursday of the Third Week of Advent

"The Spirit of the Lord shall rest upon him: a Spirit of wisdom and of understanding, A Spirit of counsel and of strength, a Spirit of knowledge and of fear of the Lord, and his delight shall be the fear of the Lord."
– Isaiah 11. 2 – 3

The Prophet Isaiah offered a treasure trove of passages readily plundered and adapted by the Gospel writers and early Christians seeking to describe and explain their experience with and living memory of Jesus.

The Spirit. It is not just any "spirit" or the "human spirit." The Spirit is not consciousness, though consciousness is enlivened by the Spirit. It is the Spirit of Wisdom and Understanding, Counsel and Strength. It is the Spirit of God. Knowledge and Awe** rests upon and dwells within this anointed one Isaiah speaks of – a knowledge and Awe birthed by the Spirit of God.

Early Christians saw Jesus as this one who was anointed by that Spirit. So, we see here in part the beginnings of the mystery of the Trinity. For us, Jesus and Spirit tango through the unfolding days of Advent.

Their ever-deepening union of love and wisdom is an inward dance – revelation further confirmed at Jesus' baptism "the Spirit of God descending on him...and there came a voice from heaven saying, 'this is my beloved Son, in whom I take delight'" (Matthew 3.16-17), and announced by Jesus himself when he stands to read the Scroll in his hometown synagogue quoting Isaiah, "the Spirit of the Lord is upon me because he has anointed me..." (Luke 4.16 – 20).

Here is more Good News: since Jesus released the Spirit to us (John 14.26; 16.13), we can partake in the anointing and receive the Resting Gift of the Spirit bringing to us the Spirit's Wisdom and Understanding through the gifts of Counsel and Strength, birthing in us Knowledge and the Ever Deepening Awareness of Almighty God and a Feeling of Awe toward God's Reality, Love and Ever-Expanding Universe in which we call home. I

In the same way you know a tree by its fruits, so too we know the anointing of the Spirit by its fruits: "love, joy, peace, patience, kindness, generosity, faithfulness, gentleness, and self-control..." (Galatians 5.22-23). These are the enduring gifts of Christmas.

Friday of the Third Week of Advent

"John was a burning and shining lamp, and for a while you were content to rejoice in his light. But I have testimony greater than John's. The works that the Father gave me to accomplish, these works that I perform testify on my behalf that the Father has sent me."
– John 5.35 – 26

We are here to develop. Here to grow. It is easy to stop growing. And it is normal to neglect or reject the possibility of growth. It is easier to eat, drink, shop and be merry, and forget about growing until New Year's resolutions.

Grow into what? We have all sorts of options to choose how we grow. In knowledge. In ignorance. In wealth. In debt. In bitterness. In joy. In productivity. In laziness. In discipline. In gluttony. In charity. In greed. In cold-heartedness. In warm-hearted love. It is easy to see that our lives grow into our choices. We literally become what do.

In the passage above, Jesus reflects on the role John played. John's was a certain quality and intensity of light. But a greater light emerges from it. Light begets light.

Light is an indication of an answer to the question what are we to grow into? We are here to develop in "the light." All life on the surface of planet earth grows in, by, through and toward the light. Scientist call it heliotropism. The tendency of living things to turn toward the light.

In a similar way, our life emanates a quality of light. We are invited to step in the journey of Grace and be transformed by the light of Christ's love into the light of Christ-love. This happens in very specific and subtle ways.

Instead of reacting so quickly with anger or profanity toward someone, we notice that we don't react at all. Instead of staying up and watching late night, we go to bed earlier and get up to pray. Instead of holding on to our money with fear, we bless others freely – even unexpectedly, realizing that God's love has always met all our needs.

Other examples and stories abound that verify that we are given models in scripture to inspire our own development and growth. John demonstrates the purpose of a lifetime is to live in, for and toward the light of the World. We don't have to create the light. We get to receive and delight in being lived by the light.

Delight. Delight. Delight. De light of the world is in you.

Saturday and Sunday of the Third Week of Advent

"Justice shall flower in his days, and profound peace, till the moon be no more. May he rule from sea to sea, and from the River to the ends of the earth."
– Psalm 72.7 – 8

Christmas is a solar event. The early church fused the story of Jesus' birth with pre-existent cultural and religious practices, as well as astronomical observations, such as the Winter Solstice. Christmas is a feast of the light(s).

The story of Jesus as the light of the world helped articulate just what it meant for the Sun to rise again on the winter horizon on December 25th, having seemingly stood in place for three days after the solstice December 21st. The ancient principle is that as it is above, so it is below. Meaning that there is a correspondence between cosmology and history. Another way of saying this is that the heavens are declaring the glory of God. One would want to know.

The scripture passage above teaches us several things, one of which is the wisdom that the moon will be replaced by the sun. A peculiar idea indeed. Yet, allegorically applied, the moon represents everything in us that is instinctual, mechanical, half-alive, perhaps even our more animal nature, half-evolved, still emerging up the layers of consciousness. The sun represents what we are to become. Fullness of life. Wholeness of being in Christ, son of God.

Life is a solar event. Not just grounded in photosynthesis. But the light of wisdom and love. The light of Christ. The light of Spirit infused and blazing in all the revelations of God to humankind – including the revelation of the creation.

At Christmas, we have a story that demonstrates the divine intention(s) of transforming the universe and our little lives into the light of love, by the light of love, through the light of love, for the light of love. How this invitation and demonstration has been distorted into shopping is perhaps something only the moon and our willingness to be lulled to sleep by its reflected, dimmed light can answer.

Monday of the Fourth Week of Advent

"But the angel said to him, 'Do not be afraid, Zechariah, because your prayer has been heard. Your wife Elizabeth will bear you a son, and you shall name him John.'"
– Luke 1.13

The daily lectionary readings for the fourth and final week of Advent leading up to Christmas Eve provide a laser focus on the birth-announcements of John and Jesus.

It's as if the church is invited to ponder the feminine role in the story of divine grace toward humankind. In the lineage of Eve, Elizabeth and Mary play leading roles in the unfolding evolution of monotheistic understanding transforming into the revelation of trinitarian mystery. Perhaps this is a nod to the feminine essence of Ruah-Spirit. Birthing life on planet earth, spiritually and biologically.

A careful reading of the Gospel reading for today (Luke 1.5- 25), will reveal that the question of John's origins are left in question. Is John, like Jesus, also from the Holy Spirit? One can deduce that Elizabeth was overshadowed by the Spirit, though the text is silent on the matter.

The main point of the announcement to Zechariah by the Angel is to confirm that God is on the move again in Israel. We can see this more clearly when the story of Zechariah and Elizabeth is paired with the promise of the Angel of the Lord to Samson's mother, which today's lectionary does (Judges 13). Samson is a type: the man of God dedicated to divine service and empowered by the Spirit. Elijah is also in the line of this type. So too, John the Baptist.

Such sacred pairings invite us to ponder the principle of spiritual receptivity that transforms all manner of duality experienced in this life, into deeper wholeness:

Elizabeth and Mary.

Zechariah and Joseph.

John and Jesus.

Body and Soul.

Light and Love.

God is always on the move. Like incense arising in the advent stillness, our gentle consent in the silence creates a space of receptivity within us to receive the Presence and partake in the mystery of Christ forming in us.

Tuesday of the Fourth Week of Advent

"Then the angel said to her, 'Do not be afraid, Mary, for you have found favor with God. Behold, you will conceive in your womb and bear a son, and you shall name him Jesus.'"
– Luke 1.30 – 31

"And behold, Elizabeth, your relative, has also conceived a son in her old age, and this is the sixth month for her who was called barren; for nothing will be impossible for God."
– Luke 1.36 – 37

We see in the Christmas story the promise of new beginnings. Here are two primary recipients of such promises: Mary, a young woman, and Elizabeth, a late middle-aged woman. And, implicit in their new beginnings, is Israel's long-hoped for new beginning too.

What speaks to me in these lines of scripture is the principle of pairing. We need each other. God works through relationships, and miracles can occur when we stick together. When we are paired with a friend. A partner. A spouse. Even, a pet.

Fear is a normal response to the ordinary and surprising events of life. And being alone is a source of fear for many. That is one reason the power of pairing is so important. And it is this feminine companionship, Mary and Elizabeth, that perhaps sustained both of these unsuspecting mothers through their season of fear, wondering and waiting.

Even in solitude, we can pair with the Presence of Love. This pairing is primary. And from this, it often happens, that other pairings emerge beyond our solitude. We draw to ourselves a friend. A companion. A miracle of personal presence. And in many ways, it is the gift of pairing that is the miracle of Christmas.

The pairing of the divine energy with the human energy in the Jesus-being. This pairing occurred not just to put Jesus in the museum of religion, or the sacristy of the church, but more so to demonstrate the possible pairing for all people, re-connecting our awareness of conscious union with and in the living God.

Wherever this union occurs for anyone in any faith or any time or culture, that mystery of union – is Christ.

Fear not. Pair up.

Wednesday of the Fourth Week of Advent

"When Elizabeth heard Mary's greeting,
the infant leaped in her womb,
and Elizabeth, filled with the Holy Spirit,
cried out in a loud voice and said,
"Most blessed are you among women,
and blessed is the fruit of your womb.
And how does this happen to me,
that the mother of my Lord should come to me?
For at the moment the sound of your greeting
reached my ears,
the infant in my womb leaped for joy.
Blessed are you who believed
that what was spoken to you by the Lord
would be fulfilled."
– Luke 1.41 – 45

Today is the Winter Solstice. In the time of Jesus, it was believed that the Winter Solstice occurred around January 6th. This astronomical and calendar miscalculation has since been corrected, but it is one of the reasons why the early church marked Jesus' birth as January 6th.

Throughout human history, the Winter Solstice was a sacred time for many religious cultures and the rising of the sun was a natural connection point with the Christian story of Jesus. When Jesus was born probably doesn't matter.

But the cosmological associations with the sun are very important and reinforce the theological valuation of Jesus' son-ship.

In modern times, the Western church now celebrates Epiphany on January 6th. However, many in the Eastern Orthodox communion still celebrate Christmas not on December 25th, but on January 6th/7th.

One application for us today is to get more in sync with the rhythms of the earth and supplement our spiritual life with them. For example, why not mark the Solstice with intention, as a way to consciously connect with the life-giving energy of the Christ-event.

The sun and its stillness on the Southern horizon for three days reminds us of the vulnerability we have without its warmth and energy. The sun is a profound analogy and metaphor for the Living Christ.

In Christ, we are compelled to become more of a solar people. Living in and by the golden light of divine love and wisdom. Yes, in a way it is all poetic. But it is also profoundly beautiful, and on this planet with this species, who doesn't need more beauty in their life? My sense is we all could benefit from being transformed more into and by the beauty of divine light and love; transformed from self-absorbed moons, into radiating, self-giving suns.

Take time tonight at dusk. Notice the cosmos and the place you exist in it. Observe the quality of light. Take time to slow down and be still and feel into the mystery of all existence and the grace of golden sunlight and warmth. I hope to do so on top of Enchanted Rock in the hill country of Central Texas, where with Elizabeth and Mary, my heart will leap at the final flash of light at the crest of southern tilt that is the Winter Solstice.

Thursday of the Fourth Week of Advent

"Mary remained with Elizabeth about three months and then returned to her home."
– Luke 1.56

We continue the theme of spiritual companionship. I referred to this companionship in Tuesday's reflection as pairing. Mary and Elizabeth, Jesus and John, are paired for purpose. They support one another in playing their roles in the unfolding story of divine love for humankind.

The insight that speaks to me is that their immediate proximity to each other only seems to have lasted for about three months, and then Mary departed. This is intriguing because it indicates that an aspect of all spiritual companionship is that it does not need to occur in person indefinitely. There is a coming together for a period of time, and then a departing for one's own "home."

Presumably, Mary arrived at Elizabeth's in the sixth month of Elizabeth's pregnancy. Staying for three months, probably means that Mary was present for John's birth, even helping Elizabeth through it. If so, that means as a new-born, John met Mary. Perhaps Mary even held John in her arms – heart to heart – not only with her's, but also Jesus's, growing in Mary's womb.

Solitude on the spiritual journey is vital. But so too is spiritual companionship. We can't do this alone. We need each other. Blessed is the person who finds a spiritual friend. Even more so, a spiritual father or mother. And most of all a spiritual companion, paired soul to soul. Such is a most meaningful Christmas gift to receive and give.

Friday of the Fourth Week of Advent

"When the time arrived for Elizabeth to have her child, she gave birth to a son."
– Luke 1.57

The lectionary and the church complete the Advent journey with the remembrance of John's birth. A day before Christmas Eve, Part One of the symphonic movement of Spirit that is Christmas, reaches is final notes: the birth of John the Baptist. The final notes of Part Two will sound forth Christmas day morning, with the familiar lines, "The people who walked in darkness have seen a great light; upon those who dwelt in the land of gloom a light has shone."
– Isaiah 9.1

But today, the Advent Remedy revels in the Forerunner. The Announcer. The Hairy Baptist. Admittedly, the cast of Christmas characters is less important than is the spiritual principles involved. So, what might those be?

John represents at least two principles. First, the importance of spiritual partnerships. in life and ministry. Second, the closure of the Prophetic lineage and the capstone of the Levitical Priesthood. Both aspects complement and precede the birth of the new thing that is trying to happen in the Christ-event. Like a double-helix, life supports life. John and Jesus. Mary and Elizabeth. Old and New.

A Rilke poem brings this home to our hearts, and invites us into the Christmas mystery, deeper and deeper:

You...go to the limits of your longing.

Embody me.

Flare up like flame and make big shadows I can move in.

For us and our healing, perhaps John represents the purifying fire of grace in Word and Silence, undoing us so to heal us. Jesus represents the light of union, the fruit of our being furrowed by the birthing fire, up through the shadows of night into the light of the cosmic body breathing in and underneath and through our layers of being.

Christmas Eve

"You, my child, shall be called the prophet of the Most High, for you will go before the Lord to prepare his way, to give his people knowledge of salvation by the forgiveness of their sins. In the tender compassion of our God the dawn from on high shall break upon us, to shine on those who dwell in darkness and the shadow of death, and to guide our feet into the way of peace."
– Luke 1.76 – 79

Our Advent journey concludes with the Christmas Eve vigil.

The dawn that breaks from on high isn't just spiritual poetry. It is the evolution of human consciousness among us in the form of John and Jesus, both emergents unfolding for our evolution as a species, despite the latent Herod-tendencies among and within us toward fear, violence and division: all dynamics that have so consistently plagued our tenure on this planet, keeping us in darkness, shadow and persistent anxiety.

John and Jesus, Mary and Elizabeth are written into the story of our human family to help us. They are here to show us who we are and what we can become. The real question is which pattern will we choose to follow. Which template will shape our life?

No one is perfect. In failure and suffering, we often discover our woundedness and see our need for inner healing and ongoing efforts toward development of being.

In "failures", we can more clearly understand our need for liberation from the darkness within us. In our times of humiliation over our behaviors, we can more clearly see how our primal reactivity and unconscious desires do not serve love, wisdom or our highest good.

So, let's be honest. Christmas Eve is less about our cultural habits of celebration and the getting and giving of gits. It is mostly about seeing the humble remedy God has initiated into the human drama not just to give us a religious ritual, but to remedy our very depth of being.

The light the scriptures speak of is here to do a work within us. Oftentimes a fierce work.

The light has dawned and will always dawn in any person who seeks for help in our all too human condition. Just ask for the help to come to you. It may surprise you how help comes at the speed of light.

So, today though we might be more predisposed to feeling nostalgic, the question remains as in every other day of the year: will we case our striving after stuff, success and substances?

Will we admit we have spent too much of our life energy and time bemused by our addictions, chasing entertainment and pleasure, losing our minds in mass sporting events, or addictions that numb our pain and dull our minds, ensnaring us to the lower impulses of these shadow-lands of our own making?

For the life of me, I can't figure out how in America, our holy days have become so much about watching grown men in spandex hit each other and throw a leather ball so that another can catch it and put it across a white line, and then celebrate as if they have just saved the world!

Is this really what humankind is here on this earth for? Scoring? I enjoy watching a game every now and then, but is this how we wish to spend our family time? Is the new shiny car or watch or whatever you might want to buy or score, really the purpose for your presence on this earth?

In contrast, witness Mary. Vessel of Love. Temple of Wisdom. Womb of Presence. Consenting to Mystery. Light Bearer. Love Deliverer. Could she perhaps have something to teach us? Could Mary's trusting be a clue to the meaning of our existence? An alternative to our endless addiction to keeping score, winning, getting, defending?

Christmas Day

"In the beginning was the Word,
and the Word was with God,
and the Word was God. He was in the beginning
with God. All things came to be through him,
and without him nothing came to be.
What came to be through him was life,
and this life was the light of the human race; the
light shines in the darkness,
and the darkness has not overcome it."
– John 1. 1 – 5

Merry Christmas.   And thank you for accompanying me on this Advent Remedy.

May our Advent preparations bear deep fruit through our silent listening during the next thirteen days of Christmas.

And let us see how Christ emerges in our hearts and being more and more as Epiphany.

Only Love In Christ.

Made in the USA
Monee, IL
13 November 2020

47421189R00049